ABC'S OF AGING

ABC'S OF AGING

Willow Creek Press®

Published by Willow Creek Press, Inc.
P.O. Box 147, Minocqua, Wisconsin 54548

Photo Credits:
p2 © Dirk Freder/iStock; p6 © Sean Mahoney/agefotostock.com; p9 © Matt Mosh/agefotostock.com;
p10 © Cyril Ruoso/Minden Pictures; p13 © Fotofeeling/agefotostock.com; p14 © Tui De Roy/Minden Pictures;
p17 © Klein-Hubert/kimballstock.com; p18 © Suzi Eszterhas/Minden Pictures; p21 © Martin Harvey/kimballstock.com;
p22 © Bernd Rohrschneider/agefotostock.com; p25 © Mark Carwardine/Minden Pictures;
p26 © Sean Crane/Minden Pictures; p29 © Thomas Marent/Minden Pictures; p30 © Ingo Arndt/Minden Pictures;
p33 © Donald M. Jones/Minden Pictures; p34 © Cyril Ruoso/Minden Pictures; p37 © Savas Sener/agefotostock.com;
p38 © Tom & Pat Leeson/KimballStock; p41 © gemredding/iStock; p42 © Kltchin & Hurst/Kimball Stock;
p45 © Mitsuaki Iwago/Minden Pictures; p46 © Richard Stacks/Kimball Stock; p49 © Klein-Hubert/kimballstock.com;
p50 © Wildlife GmbH/kimballstock.com; p53 © Lauri Tammik/agefotostock.com; p54 © MEF13/iStock;
p57 © Ian Mears/agefotostock.com; p58 © John Lund/Stephanie Roeser/agefotostock.com;
p61 © Anup Shah/NPL/Minden Pictures; p62 © Zheng Zhang/agefotostock.com; p65 © Kltchin & Hurst/Kimball Stock;
p66 © Misja Smits/Buiten-beeld/Minden Pictures; p69 © altedart/iStock; p70 © Ingo Arndt/Minden Pictures;
p73 © Dgwildlife/iStock; p74 © Suzi Eszterhas/Minden Pictures; p77 © Florian Redlinghaus/agefotostock.com;
p78 © Andy Rouse/NPL/Minden Pictures; p81 © Michel Bury/agefotostock.com; p82 © Thibault Bunoust/agefotostock.com;
p85 © Juan-Carlos Munoz/Biosphoto/Minden Pictures; p86 © Dirk Freder/iStock; p89 © Yukihiro Fukuda/NPL/Minden Pictures;
p90 © haveseen/iStock; p93 © Suzi Eszterhas/agefotostock.com; p94-95 © Eric Baccega/NPL/Minden Pictures;

Printed in China

[A]

ad·age [ad-ij] *n*. Old age and treachery will always beat youth and exuberance.
—*David Mamet*

aged [ey-jid] *adj*. Age is no barrier. It's a limitation you put on your mind.
—*Jackie Joyner-Kersee*

aging [eyj-ing] *vb*. You know you're getting old when all the names in your black book have M.D. after them.
—*Harrison Ford*

adapt [uh-dapt] *vb*. I'm at the age where food has taken the place of sex in my life. In fact, I've just had a mirror put over my kitchen table.
—*Rodney Dangerfield*

af·flic·tion [uh-flik-shuh n] *n*. Youth is a disease from which we all recover.
—*Dorothy Fuldheim*

a·lert [uh-lurt] *vb*. Be on the alert to recognize your prime at whatever time of your life it may occur.

—*Muriel Spark*

am·bi·tion [am-bish-uh n] *n*. At the age of six I wanted to be a cook. At seven I wanted to be Napoleon. And my ambition has been growing steadily ever since.

—*Salvador Dali*

a·nal·o·gous [uh-nal-uh-guh s] *adj*. Old age is like a plane flying through a storm. Once you're aboard, there's nothing you can do.

—*Golda Meir*

ap·pear [uh-peer] *vb*. Wisdom doesn't necessarily come with age. Sometimes age just shows up all by itself.

—*Tom Wilson*

ap·pear·ance [uh-peer-uh ns] *n*. Aging is a fact of life. Looking your age is not.

—*Dr. Howard Murad*

ap·pre·ci·a·tion [uh-pree-shee-ey-shuh n] *n*. I'm the same person I was back then, a little less hair, a little less chin. A lot less lungs and much less wind. But ain't I lucky I can still breathe in.

—*Maya Angelou*

art [ahrt] *n*. What if we think of aging as an art? An effort called out of the soul that takes skill, guts and devotion to manifest with the power to create laughter, seriously tweak stereotypes, and inspire?

—*Sophia Luman*

as·cend [uh-send] *vb*. Old age is like climbing a mountain. You climb from ledge to ledge. The higher you get, the more tired and breathless you become, but your views become more extensive.

—*Ingmar Bergman*

au·tumn [aw-tuh m] *n*. My garden shall yet hang heavy with tardy bloom. I shall pluck the fig in its late ripeness. The sumac will crimson for me in the frost of the fall. I shall gather wild grapes in their empurpling, and come with wild hops torn from the tops of frost-touched trees. I shall gather myself in great, ripe, yellow sheaves of me, in great clusters of maturity.

—*Muriel Strode*

a·ware [uh-wair] *adj*. As you get older you feel you need to pay more attention to what is around you and relish it. I'm greedy for beauty.

—*Bill Nighy*

[B]

baf·fle [baf-uh l] *n*. Inside every older person is a young person wondering what the hell happened.

—*Cora Harvey Armstrong*

base·ball [beys-bawl] *n*. It's like this: Father Time keeps pitching the years at us. We swing and miss a few. We hit a few out of the park. We try not to take any called strikes.

—*Robert Brault*

beau·ti·ful [byoo-tuh-fuh l] *adj*. Beautiful young people are accidents of nature, but beautiful old people are works of art.

—*Eleanor Roosevelt*

be·wil·der [bih-wil-der] *vb*. By the time we're ready to admit we've reached middle age, we're beyond it.

—*Unknown*

bi·fur·cate [bahy-fer-keyt] *vb*. 1. Forty is the old age of youth; fifty is the youth of old age.

-Victor Hugo.

bit·ter [bit-er] *adj*. There is absolutely nothing to be said in favor of growing old. There ought to be legislation against it.

—*Patrick Moore*

blur [blur] *vb*. Middle age went by while I was mourning for my lost youth.

—*Mason Cooley*

bois·ter·ous [boi-ster-uh s, -struh s] *adj*. Why would you want to grow old gracefully? Go out kicking and screaming. Stay fit, fun and kick ass 'til you die!

—*Larry Winget*

[C]

ca·pit·u·late [kuh-pich-uh-leyt] *vb*. Surrender to what is. Let go of what was. Have faith in what will be.

—*Sonia Rocotti*

chal·lenge [chal-inj] *vb*. The great challenge of adulthood is holding on to your idealism after you lose your innocence.

—*Bruce Springsteen*

chance [chans, chahns] *n*. The first half of life consists of the capacity to enjoy without the chance. The last half consists of the chance without the capacity.

—*Mark Twain*

change [cheynj] *vb*. It is never too late to be what you might have been.

—*George Eliot*

cheer·ful [cheer-fuh l] *adj*. Do not regret growing old. It is a privilege denied to many.

—*Unknown*

chil·dren [chil-druh n] *n*. Children are a great comfort in your old age—and they help you reach it faster, too.

—*Lionel Kaufmann*

col·lect [kuh-lekt] *vb.* The great thing about getting older is that you don't lose all the other ages you've been.
—*Madeleine L'Engle*

con·jec·ture [kuh n-jek-cher] *n.* Death is caused by swallowing small amounts of saliva over a long period of time.
—*George Carlin*

com·pre·hend [kom-pri-hend] *vb.* In youth we learn; in age we understand.
—*Marie von Ebner-Eschenbach*

con·tent·ment [kuh n-tent-muh nt] *n.* The mind that is wise mourns less for what age takes away; than what it leaves behind.
—*William Wordsworth*

con·tin·ue [kuh n-tin-yoo] *vb.* You are never too old to set another goal or to dream a new dream.
—*C.S. Lewis*

con·ti·nu·ity [kon-tn-oo-i-tee, -tn-yoo] *n*. There still is no cure for the common birthday.
—*John Glenn*

cost [kawst, kost] *n*. Age is a very high price to pay for maturity.
—*Tom Stoppard*

cra·zy [krey-zee] *adj*. You simply can't get to be wise, mature, etc., unless you've been a raving cannibal for thirty years or so.
—*Doris Lessing*

cre·a·tiv·i·ty [kree-ey-tiv-i-tee] *n*. There is a fountain of youth; it is your mind, your talents, the creativity you bring to your life and the lives of the people you love. When you learn to tap this source, you will truly have defeated age.
—*Sophia Loren*

cul·prit [kuhl-prit] *n.* Growing old is like being increasingly penalized for a crime you have not committed.

—*Anthony Powell*

cu·ri·os·i·ty [kyoo r-ee-os-i-tee] *n.* Don't try to be young. Just open your mind. Stay interested in stuff. There are so many things I won't live long enough to find out about, but I'm still curious about them.

—*Betty White*

cur·sive [kur-siv] *n.* If wrinkles must be written upon our brows, let them not be written upon the heart. The spirit should never grow old.

—*James A. Garfield*

cute [kyoot] *adj.* When grace is joined with wrinkles, it is adorable. There is an unspeakable dawn in happy old age.

—*Victor Hugo*

[D]

daft [daft, dahft] *n.* Of all the things I've lost, I miss my mind the most.
—*Ozzy Osbourne*

debt [det] *n.* The excesses of our youth are drafts upon our old age, payable with interest, about thirty years after date.
—*Charles Caleb Colton*

de·vel·op·ment [dih-vel-uh p-muh nt] *n.* Aging is not lost youth but a new stage of opportunity and strength.
—*Betty Friedan*

dis·il·lu·sion·ment [dis-i-loo-zhuh n] *n.* The older I grow the more I distrust the familiar doctrine that age brings wisdom.
—*H.L. Mencken*

doze [dohz] *vb.* Regular naps prevent old age, especially if you take them while driving.
—*Unknown*

dread [dred] *vb.* Aging is a slowing down of everything except fear.
—*Unknown*

[E]

ease [eez] *n.* Know that you are the perfect age. Each year is special and precious, for you shall only live it once. Be comfortable with growing older.

—*Louise Hay*

ed·u·cate [ej-oo-keyt] *vb.* Old age and the passage of time teach all things.

—*Sophocles*

ef·fort·less [ef-ert-lis] *adj.* It gets easier as you get older. You accept yourself for who you are—your flaws and attributes. It's easier to live in your own skin.

—*Barbra Streisand*

el·e·gance [el-i-guh ns] *n.* Elegance is the only beauty that never fades.

—*Audrey Hepburn*

ep·i·cure [ep-i-kyoo r] *n.* If you're covered with strange spots and smell funny, it means you're aging like a fine cheese.

—*Unknown*

e·volve [ih-volv] *vb.* 1. Aging is an extraordinary process whereby you become the person that you aways should have been.

—*David Bowie*

ex·am·ple [ig-zam-puh l] *n.* I want to get old gracefully. I want to have good posture. I want to be healthy and be an example to my children.

—*Sting*

ex·cep·tion [ik-sep-shuh n] *n.* To get back my youth I would do anything in the world, except take exercise, get up early, or be respectable.

—*Oscar Wilde*

[F]

face [feys] *n.* I think your whole life shows in your face and you should be proud of that.
—*Lauren Bacall*

faith [feyth] *n.* Even to your old age and gray hairs I am he, I am he who will sustain you. I have made you and I will carry you; I will sustain you and I will rescue you.
—*Isaiah 46:4*

fear (feer) *n.* At my age flowers scare me.
—*George Burns.*

fel·o·ny [fel-uh-nee] *n.* Youth is a wonderful thing. What a crime to waste it on children.
—*George Bernard Shaw*

fib [fib] *n.* No woman should ever be quite accurate about her age. It looks so calculating.
—*Oscar Wilde*

flip [flip] *vb*. Middle age is when your broad mind and narrow waist begin to change places.

—*E. Joseph Cossman*

for·ty [fawr-tee] *n*. Once we hit forty, women only have about four taste buds left: one for vodka, one for wine, one for cheese, and one for chocolate.

—*Gina Barreca*

fright [frahyt] *n*. True terror is to wake up one morning and discover that your high school class is running the country.

—*Kurt Vonnegut*

fur·nish·ings [fur-ni-shing] *n*. Like a lot of fellows around here, I have a furniture problem. My chest has fallen into my drawers.

—*Billy Casper*

[G]

goal [gohl] *n.* Create a life you don't need a vacation from.
—*Unknown*

gov·ern [guhv-ern] *vb.* Don't let your age control your life. Let your life control your age.
—*Anthony Douglas Williams*

grace [greys] *n.* I prefer to be a beautiful woman of my age than try desperately to look thirty.
—*Demi Moore*

grav·i·ty [grav-i-tee] *n.* I recently had my annual physical examination, which I get once every seven years, and when the nurse weighed me, I was shocked to discover how much stronger the Earth's gravitational pull has become since 1990.
—*Dave Barry*

grouch [grouch] *n.* You spend the first two thirds of your life asking to be left alone and the last third not having to ask.
—*Robert Brault*

[H]

hom·age [hom-ij] *n*. Aging has a wonderful beauty and we should have respect for that.
—*Eartha Kitt*

home·sick [hohm-sik] *adj*. Age is a foreign land I can't get used to. I want to go back home.
—*Terri Guillemets*

hope·ful [hohp-fuh l] *adj*. To keep the heart unwrinkled, to be hopeful, kindly, cheerful, reverent—that is to triumph over old age.
—*Jean Paul*

hush [huhsh] *n*. The first sign of maturity is the discovery that the volume knob also turns to the left.
—*Jerry M. Wright*

[I]

in·dul·gence [in-duhl-juh ns] *n*. The problem with people who have no vices is that generally you can be pretty sure they're going to have some pretty annoying virtues.
—*Elizabeth Taylor*

ig·nore [ig-nawr, -nohr] *vb*. The key to successful aging is to pay as little attention to it as possible.
—*Judith Regan*

in·cred·u·lous [in-krej-uh-luh s] *adj*. I am suddenly ten years older than I was, it seems, one year ago.
—*Heidi Julavits*

in·cum·bent [in-kuhm-buh nt] *adj*. Nature gives you the face you have at twenty; it is up to you to merit the face you have at fifty.
—*Coco Chanel*

in·ev·i·ta·ble [in-ev-i-tuh-buh l] *n.* Everything happens to everybody sooner or later if there is time enough.

—*George Bernard Shaw*

in·fla·tion [in-fley-shuh n] *n.* Inflation is when you pay fifteen dollars for the ten-dollar haircut you used to get for five dollars when you had hair.

—*Sam Ewing*

i·ro·ny [ahy-ruh-nee] *n.* You're never too old. Unfortunately, you're always too young to know it.

—*Robert Brault*

ir·rel·e·vant [ih-rel-uh-vuh nt] *vb.* Age is irrelevant. Ask me how many sunsets I've seen, hearts I've loved, trips I've taken, or concerts I've been to. That's how old I am.

—*Joelle*

[J]

jack·pot [jak-pot] *n.* Marry a man your own age; as your beauty fades, so will his eyesight.

— *Phyllis Diller*

ja·ded [jey-did] *adj.* The aging process has you firmly in its grasp if you never get the urge to throw a snowball.

—*Doug Larson*

jer·o·bo·am [jer-uh-boh-uh m] *n.* One should always be drunk. That's all that matters... But with what? With wine, with poetry, or with virtue, as you choose. But get drunk.

—*Charles Baudelaire*

joy [joi] *n.* "Old times" never come back and I suppose it's just as well. What comes back is a new morning every day in the year, and that's better.

—*George E. Woodberry*

[K]

kib·itz·er [kib-it-ser] *n*. This is the time when you can sit back and offer the same advice to others that you never followed in your own life.
—*Unknown*

ki·net·ic [ki-net-ik] *adj*. A man growing old becomes a child again.
—*Sophocles*

kin·ship [kin-ship] *n*. A bittersweet season: caring for our aging parents—and ourselves.
—*Jane Gross*

know·ledge [nol-ij] *n*. It is only possible to live happily-ever-after on a day-to-day basis.
—*Margaret Bonnano*

[L]

laugh·ter [laf-ter] *n.* You don't stop laughing because you grow older, you grow older because you stop laughing.
—*Maurice Chevalier*

left·o·vers [left-oh-ver] *n.* When men grow virtuous in their old age, they only make a sacrifice to God of the devil's leavings.
—*Jonathan Swift*

leth·ar·gy [leth-er-jee] *n.* Up sluggard, and waste not life; in the grave will be sleeping enough.
—*Ben Franklin*

lim·i·ta·tions [lim-i-tey-shuh n] *n.* Never put an age limit on your dreams.
—*Dara Torres*

lit·er·a·ture [lit-er-uh-cher] *n.* Some day you will be old enough to start reading fairy tales again.
—*C.S. Lewis*

love·ly [luhv-lee] *adj.* The beauty of a woman with passing years only grows.
—*Audrey Hepburn*

[M]

man·age [man-ij] *vb.* Aging is out of your control. How you handle it, though, is in your hands.
—*Diane Von Furstenberg*

mar·riage [mar-ij] *n.* When you retire you switch bosses. From the one who hired you to the one who married you.
—*Gene Perret*

math·e·mat·ics [math-uh-mat-iks] *n.* I'm sixty-five and I guess that puts me in with the geriatrics. But if there were fifteen months in every year, I'd only be forty-eight.
—*James Thurber*

meas·ure·ment [mezh-er-muh nt] *n.* The mind of a man, his brain and nerves, are a truer index of his age than the calendar.
—*Percy Bysshe Shelley*

mem·o·ry [mem-uh-ree] *n.* When I was younger, I could remember anything, whether it happened or not. Soon I shall be so that I cannot remember any but the things that never happened.
—*Mark Twain*

mem·o·ries [mem-uh-rees] *n*. The laughter and the tears, the shadows of misty yesteryears, the good times and the bad you've seen, and all the others in between, remember, do you remember the times of your life.

—*lyric, Times of Your Life*

mi·grate [mahy-greyt] *vb*. Some people, no matter how old they get, never lose their beauty—they merely move it from their faces into their hearts.

—*Martin Buxbaum*

mis·con·cep·tion [mis-kuh n-sep-shuh n] *n*. That is the great fallacy; the wisdom of old men. They do not grow wise. They grow careful.

—*Ernest Hemingway*

mis·use [mis-yooz] *vb*. I look back on the time I've wasted, and I'm just glad I wasted it while I still had the chance.

—*Robert Brault*

mo·ment (moh-muh nt) *n.*
The other day a man asked me
what I thought was the best day
of my life. "Why," I answered
without a single thought, "now."
—*David Grayson*

mon·ey (muhn-ee) *n.* It's nice
to get out of the rat race, but you
have to learn to get along with
less cheese.
—*Gene Perret*

mu·sic (myoo-zik) *n.* The age
of a woman doesn't mean a thing.
The best tunes are played on the
oldest fiddles.
—*Ralph Waldo Emerson*

mu·ta·ble (myoo-tuh-buh l)
adj. The great secret that all old
people share is that you really
haven't changed in seventy or
eighty years. Your body changes,
but you don't change at all.
—*Doris Lessing*

[N]

nar·ra·tive [nar-uh-tiv] *n*.
You get old and you realize there
are no answers, just stories.
—*Garrison Keillor*

nin·com·poops [nin-kuh
m-poop] *n*. Age, toward which
you draw amid the storms of life,
is nothing so dreadful. Those
who call it so have found all stag-
es of life unwelcome, thanks to
their mishandling of life, not to
a particular age.
—*Francesco Petrarca*

noon [noon] *n*. Probably the
happiest period in life most
frequently is middle age, when
the eager passions of youth are
cooled, and the infirmities of age
not yet begun; as we see that the
shadows, which are at morning
and evening so large, almost en-
tirely disappear at midday.
—*Eleanor Roosevelt*

nos·tal·gia [no-stal-juh] *n*.
One problem with gazing too
frequently into the past is that
we may turn around to find the
future has run out on us.
—*Michael Cibenko*

[O]

oc·to·ber [ok-toh-ber] *n.* A youthful old age is the rich and mellow autumn of life.
—*W.J. Hunter*

old [ohld] *adj.* Old wood best to burn, old wine to drink, old friends to trust, and old authors to read.
—*Francis Bacon*

oops [oo ps, oops] *interj.* Age does not diminish the extreme disappointment of having a scoop of ice cream fall from the cone.
—*Jim Fiebig*

op·por·tu·ni·ty [op-er-too-ni-tee] *n.* The best way to look at aging is to see it as an opportunity to leave what didn't work behind and step boldly into a brand new future.
—*Oprah*

op·ti·mist [op-tuh-mist] *n.* Middle age is the time when a man is always thinking that in a week or two he will feel as good as ever.
—*Don Marquis*

op·tions [op-shuh n] *n.* You can't help getting older, but you don't have to get old.
—*George Burns*

[P]

pain [peyn] *n.* The brain forgets much, but the lower back remembers everything.

—*Robert Brault*

per·cent·age [per-sen-tij] *n.* You spend ninety percent of your adult life hoping for a long rest, and the last ten percent trying to convince the Lord that you're actually not that tired.

—*Robert Brault*

per·pe·tu·i·ty [pur-pi-too-i-tee] *n.* Those who love deeply never grow old; they may die of old age, but they never die young.

—*Dorothy C. Fisher*

per·spec·tive [per-spek-tiv] *n.* Old age is always fifteen years older than I am.

—*Oliver Wendell Holmes*

pes·si·mist [pes-uh-mist] *n.* Age doesn't bring you wisdom, age brings you wrinkles.

—*Estelle Getty*

phases [feyz] *n.* I am now old enough to no longer have a fear of dying young.
—*Bruce Ades*

plans [plan] *vb.* People who ask me what I have planned for tomorrow probably assume I know what day of the week it is.
—*Unknown*

pleas·ure [plezh-er] *n.* There is no pleasure worth forgoing just for an extra three years in the geriatric ward.
—*John Mortimer*

prac·tice [prak-tis] *vb.* Old age is like everything else. To make a success of it, you've got to start young.
—*Theodore Roosevelt*

pre·tend [pri-tend] *vb.* If you're hung up on nostalgia, pretend today is yesterday and just go out and have one hell of a time.
—*Art Buchwald*

pre·var·i·cate [pri-var-i-keyt] *vb.* The secret to staying young is to live honestly, eat slowly, and lie about your age.

—*Lucille Ball*

priv·i·lege [priv-uh-lij, priv-lij] *n.* Women think that they failed somehow by not staying twenty-five. This is crazy to me because my belief is that it's a privilege to get older—not everybody gets to get older.

—*Cameron Diaz*

pro·gres·sion [pruh-gresh-uh n] *n.* First you forget names, then you forget faces. Next you forget to pull your zipper up, and finally, you forget to pull your zipper down.

—*Leo Rosenberg*

prom·ise [prom-is] *n.* Grow old with me. The best is yet to be.

—*Robert Browning*

[Q]

quan·ti·ta·tive [kwon-ti-tey-tiv] *adj*. Age is never so old as youth would measure it.

—*Jack London*

ques·tion [kwes-chuh n] *vb*. How old would you be if you didn't know how old you are?

—*Satchel Paige*

quit [kwit] *vb*. Age wrinkles the body. Quitting wrinkles the soul.

—*Douglas MacArthur*

quiz [kwiz] *n*. It's hard to feel middle-aged, because how can you tell how long you are going to live?

—*Mignon McLaughlin*

quiz·zi·cal [kwiz-i-kuh l] *adj*. I love aging. Why would I want to be twenty-one for the rest of my life?

—*Zoe Saldana*

[R]

re·al·i·za·tion [ree-uh-luh-zey-shuh n] *n.* I complain that the years fly past, but then I look in a mirror and see that very few of them actually got past.
—*Robert Brault*

re·bel·lious [ri-bel-yuh s] *adj.* I have reached an age where, if someone tells me to wear socks, I don't have to.
—*Albert Einstein*

rec·ol·lec·tion [rek-uh-lek-shuh n] *n.* By the time you're eighty years old you've learned everything. You only have to remember it.
—*George Burns*

re·morse [ri-mawrs] *n.* I was wrong to grow older. Pity. I was so happy as a child.
—*Antoine de Saint-Exupery*

re·sist [ri-zist] *vb.* Do not grow old, no matter how long you live. Never cease to stand like curious children before the great mystery into which we were born.
—*Albert Einstein*

re·spect [ri-spekt] *vb.*
There was no respect for youth
when I was young, and now
that I am old, there's no respect
for age. I missed it coming and
going.
—*J.B. Priestley*

ret·ro·spect [re-truh-spekt]
n. In fact, looking back, it seems
to me that I was clueless until I
was about fifty years old.

—*Nora Ephron*

re·verse [ri-vurs] *vb.* Life
would be infinitely happier if we
could only be born at the age of
eighty and gradually approach
eighteen.
—*Mark Twain*

re·wind [ree-wahynd] *vb.* You
can't turn back the clock. But
you can wind it up again.
—*Bonnie Prudden*

rule [rool] *n.* Age and glasses of
wine should never be counted.
—*Italian proverb*

[S]

sac·ri·fice [sak-ruh-fahys] *vb*. You can live to be a hundred if you give up all things that make you want to live to be a hundred.

—*Woody Allen*

sched·ule [skej-ool] *n*.
Monday—brush teeth.
Tuesday—comb hair.
Wednesday—cut nails.
Thursday—shower.
Friday—change clothes.
Saturday—shave.
Sunday—apply deodorant.

—*Unknown*

scheme [skeem] *vb*. When you're old, leave snacks in little bags on the floor all over the house in case you fall down.

—*Unknown*

self [self] *n*. There is no old age. There is, as there always was, just you.

—*Carol Grace*

shock [shok] *vb*. A person is always startled when he hears himself seriously called an old man for the first time.

—*Oliver Wendell Holmes*

slam·mer [slam-er] *n.* Age is a prison from which we cannot escape.

—*Morrow Bourne*

se·nil·i·ty [si-nil-i-tee] *n.* Why wait for senility? Have your second childhood now while you can still enjoy it.

—*Unknown*

soft·ware [sawft-wair] *n.* Age is like the newest version of a software—it has a bunch of great new features, but you lost all the cool features the original one had.

—*Terri Guillemets*

speed [speed] *n.* You get up one day, young, make a quick sandwich, throw back a cold beer, then BAM—you're old—just like that.

-*Terri Guillemets*

spir·it [spir-it] *n.* I'm happy to report that my inner child is still ageless.

—*James Broughton*

sports [spawrts, spohrts] *n.* It's a mere moment in a man's life between an All-Star Game and an Old-Timers Game.

—*Vin Scully*

strat·e·gy [strat-i-jee] *n.* The trick is to age honestly and gracefully and make it look great, so that everyone looks forward to it.

—*Emma Thompson*

style [stahyl] *n.* Whatever a man's age, he can reduce it several years by putting a bright-colored flower in his buttonhole.

—*Mark Twain*

sub·stance [suhb-stuh ns] *n.* I look forward to being older, when what you look like becomes less an issue and what you are is the point.

—*Susan Sarandon*

sur·prise [ser-prahyz] *vb.* Old age is the most unexpected of all things that happen to a man.

—*Leon Trotsky*

[T]

tasks [task, tahsk] *n.* Wake up in the morning with nothing to do and having done only half by bedtime.

—*Unknown*

ter·mi·nate [tur-muh-neyt] *v.* People are crazy and times are strange. I'm locked in tight, I'm out of range. I used to care, but things have changed.

—*Bob Dylan*, Things Have Changed

time [tahym] *n.* The challenge of retirement is how to spend time without spending money.

—*Unknown*

time·less [tahym-lis] *adj.* We are always the same age inside.

—*Gertrude Stein*

traf·fic [traf-ik] *n.* The elderly don't drive that badly; they're just the only ones with time to do the speed limit.

—*Jason Love*

tran·si·tion [tran-zish-uh n] *vb*. Aging is not an option, not for anyone. It is how gracefully we handle the process and how lucky we are as the process handles us.

—*Cindy McDonald*

trans·port [trans-pawrt] *vb*. To be happy, we must be true to nature and carry our age along with us.

—*William Hazlitt*

trea·sure [trezh-er] *n*. I will add each day of my life to my treasure of days lived. And with each day my treasure will grow, not diminish.

—*Robert Brault*

tu·te·lage [toot-l-ij] *n*. The years teach much which the days never knew.

—*Ralph Waldo Emerson*

[U]

um·brage [uhm-brij] *n.* Some guy said to me: "Don't you think you're too old to sing rock n' roll?" I said: "You'd better check with Mick Jagger. "

—*Cher*

un·al·ter·a·ble [uhn-awl-ter-uh-buh l] *adj.* As long as the Stones keep their hair and don't get fat, they'll get away with the wrinkles.

—*Joe Elliot*

un·chart·ed [uhn-chahr-tid] *adj.* It's strange to have children at the beginning of life and parents nearing the end.

—*Amy Waldman*

un·truth [uhn-trooth] *n.* It is utterly false and cruelly arbitrary to put all the play and learning into childhood, all the work into middle age, and all the regrets into old age.

—*Margaret Mead*

[V]

vice [vahys] *n*. When our vices desert us, we flatter ourselves that we are deserting our devices.

—*Unknown*

vic·to·ry [vik-tuh-ree] *n*. Old age is not a disease—it is strength and survivorship, triumph over all kinds of vicissitudes and disappointments, trials and illnesses.

—*Maggie Kuhn*

view·point (vyoo-point) *n*. Age is not how old you are, but how many years of fun you've had.

—*Matt Maldre*

vi·sion [vizh-uh n] *n*. God grant me the senility to forget the people I never liked anyway, the good fortune to run into the ones I do, and the eyesight to tell the difference.

—*Ron Sims*

[W]

wall·flow·er [wawl-flou-er]
n. I could not, at any age, be
content to take my place in a
corner by the fireside and simply
look on.
-*Eleanor Roosevelt*

ward·robe [wawr-drohb] *n.*
Old age is a blessed time. It gives
us leisure to put off our earthly
garments one by one, and dress
ourselves for heaven.
—*Elizabeth Missing Sewell*

wea·ry [weer-ee] *vb.* Life is
one long process of getting tired.
—*Samuel Butler*

words [wurd] *n.* It's the rudest
word in my dictionary, "retire."
And "old" is another one. I don't
allow that in my house. And
being called "vintage." I don't
want any of those old words. I
like "enthusiastic."
—*Judi Dench*

[X]

xan·a·du [zan-uh-doo] *n.* We turn not older with the years, but newer every day.

—*Emily Dickinson*

[Y]

years [yeer] *n.* Trust me friend, 100 years goes faster than you think, so don't blink.
—*Kenny Chesney*, Don't Blink

yes·ter·day [yes-ter-dey] *n.* There is no distance on this earth as far away as yesterday.
—*Robert Nathan*

yield [yeeld] *vb.* Yield to temptation. It may not pass your way again.
—*Robert A. Heinlein*

youth [yooth] *n.* You are as young as your faith, as old as your doubt; as young as your self-confidence, as old as your fear; as young as your hope, as old as your despair.
—*Douglas MacArthur*

youth·ful [yooth-fuh l] *adj.* Father Time is not always a hard parent, and, though he tarries for none of his children, often lays his hand lightly upon those who have used him well.
—*Charles Dickens*

[Z]

zeal [zeel] *n*. A certain nervous disorder afflicting the young and inexperienced.

—*Ambrose Bierce*

ze·ro [zeer-oh] *n*. The ledger of my life can lean heavy with a prolific array of stellar investments, yet in the tallying I would be wise to remember that an investment that is not of God will leave a zero balance on the ledger of my life no matter how many different ways I try to add it up.

—*Craig D. Lounsbrough*